A No More Stolen Childhoods

By D. Wayne Coffey

A
No
More
Stolen
Childhoods

**ONE MAN'S COURAGEOUS FIGHT TO HEAL HIMSELF,
PROTECT ALL CHILDREN FROM SEXUAL ABUSE AND
HELP VICTIMS RECLAIM THEIR LIVES**

By D. Wayne Coffey

DEDICATION

To my wife and soul mate, Dolores,
and to my incredible children —
Kathryn, Allyson, David and Melissa

NO MORE STOLEN CHILDHOODS

Our Mission

To change the public perception about childhood sexual abuse and to help those abused find fulfillment in their permanently scarred lives.

Table of Contents

INTRODUCTION
Monty Roberts
The man who listens to horses

All of us realize that Wayne's title *No More Stolen Childhoods* is a hope. It is a prayer to God that a sense of decency will come over the world and every human being will see that each child is entitled to a safe place to live. Wayne is placing one brick in a wall against any crime perpetrated on those of us who are most vulnerable, the children. The innocence of childhood should be cherished, and with this book, Wayne Coffey is attempting to make that happen.

If the prayer that this book represents is to make a difference, it will be because thousands of individuals like Wayne Coffey will take the time to speak out. Wayne happens to be a high-performing, high-earning man who might easily take the position that he doesn't need the aggravation. It takes energy and fortitude to come forward with negative stories of one's past when there is no way to eliminate the pain, memory or certainly the act itself. Wayne Coffey mustered the courage to make a huge effort solely to help others.

— *Monty Roberts*
Flag Is Up Farms
Solvang, California

A Note to Readers

Although life is lived chronologically, it is not always remembered as such. Certain experiences take precedence over others, and certain themes pop up again and again. I have pieced together my story as neatly as possible, but, ultimately, the past unfolds in its own way. What's most important, therefore, is the story itself.

Already there are things I want to add to these pages — memories, experiences and insights keep coming. I'll have to save them for another time, however, knowing they, too, will unfold in their own way and time as my journey continues.

—D. Wayne Coffey

CHAPTER 1
The Court of No Return

May 10, 1999. Baltimore County Circuit Court.

I'm standing in the hallway, outside of the courtroom of Judge Thomas J. Bollinger. My wife, Dolores, is at my side. So is my daughter Katie and Father Ray Chase; all are here to lend me much needed support. We're waiting for Case No. 99-CR-0119 to be heard. It's taken nine months to get to this point, nine months of bureaucratic machinations and paperwork, painful memories, feelings of resolve and uncertainty.

I am present yet not present, aware of my surroundings yet not. I am nervous as hell and sweating.

Judge Bollinger has a full docket today. There will be no jury to weigh the facts, only him. He alone will determine my fate and that of countless others, the very others I am seeking to protect.

We are getting ready to enter the courtroom when suddenly I see Uncle Glen. Of all my uncles when I was growing up, he has always been my favorite. I wonder what he's doing here and then — pow — it hits me. Uncle Glen, who is an attorney, is not here to *support* me but to argue *against* me in court. He walks by with a scowl and an almost imperceptible shake of his head, as if to say, "How could you?"

I am dumbfounded and unnerved, but this is nothing compared to what I feel as I enter the courtroom. The place is packed with what feels like hundreds of people but is really only about 50 — plaintiffs, defendants, attorneys and courtroom junkies. For some reason, I assumed my case would be heard in a small private courtroom, where decorum, like justice, prevailed. Instead, it is to be tried in front of all these strangers. Will they turn and stare at me, whisper to each other as the facts of the case are presented?

Although I was the one to bring suit, it is now in the hands of the Maryland State's Attorney. Dolores, Katie, Father Chase and I are simply observers, sitting towards the back of the courtroom, on the left-hand side. I look around, searching for my mother. I cannot believe she isn't present. Although she doesn't deny the facts of the case, she refuses to acknowledge them publicly. Family secrets should stay secret, she insists, no matter how heinous they may be. But while I do not see her, I do see her sister, my Aunt Martha, who is Uncle Glen's wife. She is one row behind us but on the opposite side of the aisle. She, like Uncle Glen, is here to support the defendant, John Joseph Sprainis.

And there the defendant sits. Ten years have passed since I last saw him, but the emotions are all still there — the shame, anger and despair. I have gone too far to turn back, yet I no longer doubt I was right to bring him to court to answer for the irreparable harm he inflicted on me and, I am convinced, on others. I expect justice — that he will get what he deserves.

He is John Joseph Sprainis — my Uncle Johnny. The man who sexually abused me weekly, for years, beginning when I was five. *He is the man who stole my childhood.*

CHAPTER 2
39 Million

I, Wayne Coffey, am a statistic. I am one in the 39 million Americans who have been sexually abused before the age of 18.

If 39 million is too large a number to comprehend, think of it this way: It is larger than the combined populations of

> New York
> Los Angeles
> Chicago
> Houston
> Philadelphia
> Phoenix
> San Antonio
> Washington, DC

If the number is still too large to get your hands around, let me present it to you in another, equally graphic way:

One in four girls and one in six boys are sexually abused before they turn 18. That means that every fourth woman or sixth man you see at work or church, or at the supermarket or bus stop — will have been victimized as a child. The median age for *reported* abuse? Nine-years-old.[1]

This is not just a travesty; it is an epidemic. It makes childhood sexual abuse — the most heinous crime against children — equal to or more prevalent in number than prostate cancer (1 in 6 men) and breast cancer (1 in 8 women).

But while public awareness campaigns help pour research dollars into eradicating these devastating diseases, childhood sexual abuse remains one of the best and worst kept secrets. Ninety percent of childhood sexual abuse is committed by family members or friends of family. This makes it especially difficult, if not impossible, for victims to speak out — the shame, anger and fear are simply too great. Childhood sexual abuse also is something many of us find too uncomfortable to acknowledge, let alone comprehend.

It has taken decades for me to step forward and share my dark and painful secret. This book is part of that effort. I must tell you at the outset it is not an easy read. I will be taking you inside the very experience of abuse, not just physically but emotionally. You will see everything through my eyes, as a child and as an adult, for sexual abuse continues long after it stops; it scars you permanently. It permeates all you do and think, and how you relate to loved ones, friends and colleagues, let alone yourself.

But know, too, that something good can come of bad. With hope and support — for me, from my wife and soul mate,

---

[1] *See Appendix 2 for additional statistics on childhood sexual abuse.*

Dolores, my incredible children and my strong spiritual beliefs —
you can begin to reclaim your life and, with courage and time,
begin to trust again. In that sense, I believe my story to be
inspirational. I hope by the end of it you will agree.

CHAPTER 3
Fait Accompli

I was born in 1954, and raised in one of Baltimore's typical row houses. My parents, Roy and Urtella, had five children over a span of 10 years. Of the four sons and one daughter, I was smack in the middle.

Ours was a large extended family, at least on my mother's side. We had Grandfather and Grams, 20-plus cousins and several aunts, including my Aunt Martha. Uncle Johnny was my mother's youngest sibling, and she felt a special obligation to watch over him because he was 50 percent deaf and mildly retarded. She was, in fact, more like a mother to him, having helped raise him and her other siblings after her own mother died.

Uncle Johnny was my godfather, which was a very big deal in my family. He worked at a bookbindery back then and lived with my grandfather expense-free. That meant he could save his money and buy me great gifts. My cousins were jealous because their godparents could not do the same. Had they known the price I paid for those gifts, they would have changed their minds. Whatever the case, Uncle Johnny's generosity raised no flags for my parents.[1]

Uncle Johnny came over Fridays after work and stayed the weekend, or we would see him Sundays at my grandfather's house. It was during these weekly visits (not to mention Christmas, Thanksgiving and other special holidays) that the abuse occurred. It continued unabatedly from the time I was five until I was 13 and finally had the strength, both physically and mentally, to fend him off.

It began with fondling. He'd take me in his lap and hold me. My parents would see us but not realize what was really going on. They thought it was cute. As I got older, Uncle Johnny would take me up to his room. It was the only one with a door, so he could do whatever he wanted, unobserved.

Uncle Johnny also took me places, which my mother thought was wonderful. I guess she assumed we were spending "quality time" together. Sometimes, he'd take me to a club where other deaf men played pool or to the Holiday Fitness Center, where he worked out in the exercise room. Sometimes

---

[1] *In this sense, my parents were a lot like so many other parents and guardians. They did not recognize the warning signs of abuse. In some ways, this is easy to understand as 90 percent of the incidences of sexual abuse are committed by family members or individuals a child knows. Further, the seduction often occurs slowly, making the abuse that much more difficult to recognize. Nonetheless, as you will see in Appendix 2, warning signs do exist.*

he would just pull off the road and show me *Playboy* magazines, hoping to arouse me. Other times, he would lead me into my grandfather's musty shed, a stone's throw from the house.[2]

This happened every weekend throughout my childhood. The weekend would come and there my uncle would be. There wasn't a damn thing I could do about it. It was a fait accompli. I was an object to him, no longer a child, no longer a human being.

When I was very young, I knew that what was happening was terribly wrong, but Uncle Johnny warned me if that I told anyone I'd get in big trouble. And so I kept quiet. I would just think to myself, okay, do it, get it over with. But as I got older and more sexually aware, things got complicated. I still knew my uncle's actions were wrong, but there was pleasure in being touched. This, too, felt terribly wrong. The pleasure, the abject pain — the power of these opposing forces is impossible to describe. I felt absolutely trapped in my body and mind, controlled by someone in a position of power and authority.

These feelings still entrap me. They don't just disappear over time. I can't "just get over it." A stolen childhood isn't like a stolen purse, which can be replaced. When you live with a secret that dark, it gets ingrained in the pathways of your mind until the pathways become as deep as the Grand Canyon. To climb out of the Canyon is very, very difficult. No matter how close you get to doing it, you slip back in. And it hurts deeply.

---

[2] *Recently, that musty smell has returned. I'll be going about the business of my day when out of nowhere it rises up. It's as if I'm standing inside that shed again. Needless to say, it's disturbing, but I've found that lavender oil overpowers the smell and all others. That's the kind of oil my massage therapist uses. It smells great and relaxes me. My wife, Dolores, thinks I'm a bit crazy when I put some on my pillow, but it helps me sleep. Sleep isn't easy to come by some nights. Memories slip in, so I need all the help I can get.*

Looking back, though, I see was a lucky kid. Although I couldn't stop my uncle's abuse, at least until I got older and could fend him off, I did find a respite. That respite changed my life; you can even say it saved me: the Boy Scouts of America.

CHAPTER 4
Achegim, One Who Instructs

I know it sounds dramatic to say Boy Scouts helped save my life, but it's true for several reasons. First, Scouting made me feel good about myself. It provided ideals I could aspire to and measure myself against: self-reliance, courage, honesty, kindness, helpfulness and loyalty. I took the Scout Oath as gospel. Even today I strive to adhere to it:

> *On my honor I will do my best*
> *To do my duty to God and my country*
> *And to obey the Scout Law;*
> *To help other people at all times;*
> *To keep myself physically strong,*
> *Mentally awake, and morally straight.*

Second, Scouting helped me escape Uncle Johnny. Scout meetings were held Friday evenings, and many of my weekends and summers were devoted to camping trips and other activities. These provided a reprieve from my uncle's weekly sexual abuse. I had time to think about other things, and to be a person in my own right, not just a victim.

Third, in stark contrast to my life in the city, Scouting introduced me to a world of beauty: the great outdoors. I loved walking in the woods — the way the sun came through the trees, the sound of tree limbs snapping as I hiked, and all the smells, like the crisp morning air or food cooked over an open fire. Sleeping in a tent was so peaceful, especially when it started to rain. I also loved sitting around the campfire with my fellow Scouts. We'd sing songs, tell jokes and stories, and get into long, stimulating conversations about life. It felt good to think big thoughts and to realize there was a world beyond Uncle Johnny's reach.

As I advanced rapidly through the ranks, I took on greater responsibilities and challenges, and I excelled at them. I was elected to the Order of the Arrow, which is the equivalent of the Boy Scouts' honor society. From there, I was selected to receive the Scouts' highest honor, the Vigil Honor. Less than 2 percent of all Scouts do so.[1]

To receive the Vigil Honor, you must go through an induction, which requires that you survive on your own in the wilderness for a night and a day. You are not given any food, clothing or shelter. It's just you and the forest. Every few hours someone comes by, not to check on you as much as to ask questions designed to make you really think about your life — your strengths and goals,

---

[1] *Two years later, I was awarded the rank of Eagle Scout, which is summed up in these few words: "I am the eagle. Since the beginning of time, man has used me and my brothers as a symbol of royalty, power, victory, authority and valor." (Eagle Court of Honor Handbook)*

and how you are going to use your talents to help other people. It was a very powerful experience for me, much like the hero's journey Joseph Campbell describes in his book *The Power of Myth*.

According to Campbell, heroes only come into their own through some sort of trial. The trial can be physical: Heroes fight a courageous battle or save a life in order to reclaim something that has been taken from them. Or the trial can be spiritual: Heroes take off on a series of adventures that push them beyond ordinary ways of thinking and doing.

Looking back now, I see how I was on both types of hero journeys — one to reclaim the childhood Uncle Johnny had wrested from me and one to regain my sense of self-worth. I came away from the experience a changed person, which is not to say my scars suddenly disappeared; the scars of childhood sexual abuse never do.

Upon completing the Vigil Honor, I was bestowed with the Native American name of Achegim, meaning "One Who Instructs." This brings me to the fourth reason Scouts was so important: It taught me the invaluable leadership skills I would need throughout my life, especially in the business world.

The Scouting program in the Baltimore area had a youth leadership training program called Thunderbird, which provided opportunities to learn leadership skills and apply them at home and in the community. I thoroughly enjoyed the experience and learned much in a short time. Soon after, I was chosen — just one of 32 individuals nationwide — to teach at the Scouts national leadership training school at the Schiff Scout Reservation in Northern New Jersey. It was an honor and a thrill, especially as I was in the company of some of the smartest, most inspirational people I had ever known. Many became my mentors. I'd like to think that I, too, became a mentor to Scouts coming up through the ranks. Helping them to

reach their goals was one of the most rewarding experiences
I have ever had. And this, too, made me feel good about myself.

Today, I can't imagine where I would have been — where
I would be still — without Scouts. Likely, I would have nose-dived,
probably even become a juvenile delinquent. I had too much
energy, much of it negative, that needed channeling, especially
as I entered my teens. Friends outside of Scouting were drinking
and carrying on. They thought Scouting was for sissies and
laughed at me when — on Friday nights, no less — I headed out
to Scout meetings in my uniform and knee socks.[2] I didn't give in
to peer pressure, however. Scouting provided me with a moral
compass. It made me feel I was doing good in the world and that
maybe — *just maybe* — I was a good person.

---

[2] *I had the last laugh on my friends, however, when I dared them to go camping
with me. They quickly learned that Scouting was for anyone but sissies. Having to
find something to eat and a place to sleep in a pitch black forest filled with strange
animal sounds scared them to death.*

CHAPTER 5
My Best Worst Job

I might not be a Harvard grad, but I'd like to think I'm bright enough. One thing I can say with certainty, however, is that I love to learn. If I can read about it, I can grasp it. If I like what I learn, I become passionate about it. I credit all this to my parochial education.

I have always been a person with strong spiritual beliefs, so the parochial school environment worked well for me. More importantly, I felt challenged intellectually. My teachers were exceptional, and they had very high standards. In that sense, school was a lot like Scouts. I could push myself to my limits and excel. There was a flip side to this, of course. Sometimes I wouldn't let up. I have a Type-A personality, and I always had to go full out. In my mind, there was no second effort.

My parents had five kids to put through school. Money was tight, so I had to transfer to a public high school. I hated it. The teachers were uninspiring and the classes were too easy. My grades plummeted and I cut class (though, in my defense, I often snuck out to Baltimore's internationally renowned Walters Art Museum; anything for stimulation). However, I did join the school concert choir and ran cross-country and track. These interests kept me in school and pretty busy and, of course, there was Scouts, which kept me in line.

During this time, I pushed myself to be the "ideal kid." I spent many after-school hours mowing my neighbors' lawns and dragging their garbage cans out to the alley, hoping they'd think I was a good person. I tried to be good at home and even to be polite to Uncle Johnny. He couldn't sexually abuse me anymore. I had made a stand for myself. Still, being near him was hard. I began to distance myself from the whole experience. I wasn't blocking it out as much as trying to put it behind me. What was done, was done. Time to cover my deep wound and move on.

I didn't realize how memories of childhood sexual abuse never fade, however. As an adult, they expressed themselves as an unbridled rage that threatened my marriage and relationship with my children. As a kid, they took the form of insomnia. No matter how hard I worked or busy I kept, a kind of panic would come over me as I laid in bed at night. It was as if every negative thought I had about myself found a way to slip into the few unscheduled hours I had. I couldn't sleep and bought myself sleeping pills, hoping they would alleviate the anxiety and fears that overcame me at night. But even these didn't really help. I came to dread nighttimes.

To make money during those years, I worked at Bob's Big Boy. It was the best worst job I ever had. I began at the bottom, picking cigarette butts out of the rocks and shrubbery, and mowing the grass. Eventually I worked my way up to short order cook, which was only partly an improvement. I quit the restaurant lots of times to attend Boy Scout camp in the summer, but I always came back during school and breaks. The people were nice enough and, hey, money was money.

After a grueling summer at leadership training school the summer I was 18, I swore to myself I wouldn't work at Bob's Big Boy again, so I hit the pavement looking for other work. One night, however, that pavement happened to run right by the restaurant. I sat at the counter, sipped my coffee and chatted with Jim Joyner, the assistant manager. "We really need a cook to work 8 a.m. to 5 p.m.," he said. "What do you say?" "Sorry, Jim, but I'm moving on to bigger and better things," I replied. He nodded, we kept talking.

Jim, who was in his fifties, didn't have a lot of formal education. He had graduated from the school of hard knocks, however, and knew a lot about people. Apparently, he knew a lot about me.

"We have a bunch of new waitresses," he said casually.

I looked around. "Yeah, well they don't excite me."

"The best one's downstairs on a break."

I wasn't biting — until I saw her. "Holy cow! The 8-to-5 shift, you said? Sign me up."

And that's how I met Dolores. I knew right off that I wanted to marry her. She was seeing another guy at the time, so it was a matter of waiting him out. In the meantime, Dolores and I became very close friends. As soon my shift ended, I would run home, take a shower, go back to Bob's Big Boy and we would talk for hours. I would take her home when her shift was over, anything to spend time with her. I was madly in love. She was, as she still is, my soul mate.

We married when I was 21 and Dolores was 20. I hid from her the facts of my abuse. For the first time in my life, I could blot out the shame and fear because I had someone I loved, someone who loved me in return.

Before and right after we married, I jumped around a bit. I attended Concordia College in New York, which is the Missouri Synod's pre-seminary program. It took me all of 90 days to realize that this life was not for me. I attended Essex Community College, majored in biology and graduated summa cum lade. I then took classes at Towson State University but left my senior year.

While I was at Towson, a friend asked if I wanted to work weekends on his uncle's fruit farm. I did and fell in love yet again, this time with farming. The land, the life — they were like magnets pulling me into a challenge on par with, or even greater than, Scouting. Farming would take everything I had, physically and mentally. There'd be little time to think and, with luck, I'd be so tired at the end of the day that I'd fall right asleep. Or so I thought.

CHAPTER 6
Blow-up Sundays on the Farm

Although I wanted to buy a farm, I couldn't afford one. So I did the next best thing: I managed one. The farm belonged to T. Courtenay Jenkins, an incredible human being. He's since passed on, but I still owe much to him; he was a second father to me.

Courtenay's farm was magnificent.[1] We lived on more than 100 acres, with 125-year-old boxwood bushes, a perennial garden and breathtaking vistas. We also had an organic garden, so we always had fresh vegetables, which we also sold to health food stores in the area. At one point, we had more than 700 asparagus plants and hundreds of spring onions and heads of broccoli.

The farm in the morning was always crisp and bright. I looked forward to getting up and out very early. I lived in jeans

---

[1] *My ties to the farm remain strong. I live just a few minutes drive from it, and Dolores and I still walk around the grounds.*

and a t-shirt and, in the winter, coveralls. Even though I weighed just 120 pounds, I was wiry and in the best shape of my life. I could lift 100-pound sacks of feed and do whatever else needed to be done around the place.

I learned to be good with my hands because when something broke down, it was up to me to fix it. Our hay baler, pickup truck — I rebuilt them both. Not surprisingly, my hands were calloused from pitchforks, hay baling and general farm work.

We had 100 head of cattle, making ours the largest purebred Shorthorn farm in Baltimore County. From January through March, we delivered calves in the bowels of the barn. I had to be on call 24 hours a day, but I didn't mind. It was a great joy bringing a calf to life, but there was also sadness. Sometimes a young cow didn't take to her calf and would butt it to the point where we had to put the calf down.

Watching the summer thunderstorms roll in from 20 miles away was incredible. I would see the black and green clouds gather, being driven toward the farm by the westerly winds. I'd have to race to get all the cattle and horses into the barn for safekeeping. The barn itself was built in 1860 and had massive beams and two huge doors. I had to batten down the doors before the storm hit or else the wind would come into the barn and literally lift me off the floor.

In the summers, I would hire high school students and we'd bale over 17,000 bales of hay to feed our cattle and to sell to area horse farms. The smell of freshly mown hay was great. I still miss it to this day, just as I miss standing around at the end of the day, talking with the students about all we accomplished. It didn't matter to me that it had been nearly 95 degrees out or that it was a good 10 to 20 degrees higher on the top of a hay mow. I loved it.

My dog, Shane, followed me everywhere. He was a shepherd-collie mix and the most loyal, sweet-natured dog in the world. If I were out tracking cows, he was by my side. If I were driving out to a field, he'd hop in the back of the pick-up. I loved his company.

There was a simplicity to life that I enjoyed. We heated the house with the cords of wood I cut. We canned our own vegetables. Dolores sewed our clothes. We had a small 12" black and white TV that received only three channels, which meant we did a lot of reading and talking. We truly enjoyed each other's company (which was a good thing as our closest neighbors were nearly half a mile away). In the winter, we'd go sledding or snowmobiling. My twin girls, Katie and Allyson, were born on the farm the year we moved to it, and I loved pushing them in the tire swing as I sang Scouting songs and listening to them laugh. There's no better sound than a child's laugh. And I loved watching them pulling their little red wagon as they walked with Dolores down our half-mile tree-lined driveway to where I was working in the field, just so we could eat lunch together.

Not long after, my son David was born. He, too, loved the farm and he and his sisters would argue over who got to go with me to the stockyards or to pick up cows in the cattle truck; they were convinced it was the biggest truck on earth. At night, I often took the three of them out for a walk, to teach them that there was nothing to fear about the dark. I remember them squeezing my hands and staying close, and how good it felt to be their protector.

Melissa, my youngest daughter, was also born on the farm (though several years later, after I had stopped farming). She loved living there as much as she loved David, which is saying a lot! She followed her brother everywhere, and the two of them became inseparable, which was wonderful to see.

And so, with my family complete and Dolores and I still madly in love, I felt like I was living in Mayberry RFD — everything simple and easy.

Except, of course, it wasn't.

Whereas I once tried to prove my self-worth by being the ideal kid, I now tried to prove it by working as hard as I could, as many hours as I could. I was like an alcoholic who drinks to deaden the pain, only I did so by lifting feed bags, baling hay and rebuilding engines. But I still couldn't make the searing pain go away, nor could I find the sleep that others took for granted. I'd toss and turn, alternating between utter despair and self-loathing. My anger was like a volcano that threatened to — and often did — explode. It was as if evil spirits had taken over my body and wouldn't let go. I'm a proud man, one who wants to stay in control, but in the face of the evil spirits I didn't stand a chance.

There were times, especially after one of my explosions, when I would curl into a fetal position and just sob uncontrollably. I'd do this late at night, when I thought no one would see me. It felt horrible to lose it like that. It was even worse the times Dolores found me this way. Not only did she not know what set me off — I was like a land mine — but she didn't know why I was laying there crying. I'm sure it scared and confused her. It scared and confused me, too. I didn't realize at the time the connection between my dark moods and my sexual abuse. Even if I had, I don't know if I would have told Dolores about it. I would be too scared of her reaction. Would she view me as less of a man or stop loving me? Or worse, leave me?

I didn't have to explain anything to my dog, Shane, however. He loved me unconditionally. When I curled up on the floor, he'd lie beside me, lick my face and cry the way dogs do when you leave a room. It was as if he were telling me, "It's OK. I'm here. I'm not going to leave you. We're in this together." And we were. He truly was this man's best friend.[2]

---

[2] *One day, I came home to find Shane had been hit by a truck. That night, we buried him in the backyard. My grief was almost unbearable, but I kept it to myself.*

After such episodes in the house, I'd be mentally and physically spent. If you asked me to spell my name, I wouldn't have had the strength or ability to do so. It would take me a while to bounce back. Being in touch with nature certainly helped me do so. Nature, as I've noted, is important to my psyche. I think of it as love in its rawest, most basic form: love without human frailties. But sometimes when I was alone — and most of the day I was — my deep wounds would open and my frailties would became evident. The evil spirits would reappear and my anger would return.

I lashed out at Dolores and the children for no reason, at least none they could understand. I remember one time I was raking leaves outside the house and the more I raked, the angrier I got. Finally, I just lost it and started screaming at them about how hard I was working while they were just hanging around having a good time. I made them come out and help me rake. The children began to cry, and I immediately felt terrible. But I also felt helpless; it was as if some dark, otherworldly force had taken over. After episodes like these, Dolores would ask, almost plead, for me to tell her what was going on, but all I could say was, "I don't know."

Later, in counseling, I realized that most of my explosions occurred on Sundays. I began to refer to them as my "blow-up Sundays." When I was a boy, Sunday was the day my family visited my grandfather's house, and there would be Uncle Johnny, just waiting to take me away ... down the road ... into the shed ... . The anger I couldn't release then, I released now. Unfortunately, Dolores and the children got the brunt of it. For this I am profoundly sorry and still agonize over the hurt I caused. I've apologized to them, but nothing I say will ever fully erase the bad memories they have of me.

It pains me to say that my children — Katie and Allyson, and David and Melissa, who came later — never had the dad they wanted or deserved. In that sense they, too, had a stolen childhood. I was too angry and distant. My distance was not just emotional but physical. I didn't hug and kiss my children. I didn't hold them in my lap or roughhouse with my son, as other fathers did. I was afraid to because I knew the statistics: that the majority of sexually abused children become abusers themselves. My fear was that someone would see me being physical with my kids and accuse me of abuse. And so I held back.[3]

During those years, family would come out to the farm — my mother and father, cousins, and aunts and uncles, including Johnny. I couldn't *not* invite him to family get-togethers without revealing my reasons to everyone. But I loathed his presence — it felt like an evil spirit — but I was an adult now. I knew he would never be able to victimize me again. I thought I could leave it at that.

One time my family came out for Katie and Allyson's birthday. Photos were taken and were later shown to my grandmother. One was of Uncle Johnny, smiling into the camera, holding the twins in his lap, one girl on each of his knees. When my grandmother saw the photo, she immediately called our house and told Dolores to never let Uncle Johnny near the girls again. As it turned out, one of the female members of our family had ten years earlier admitted to my grandmother that she had been sexually abused by him. After Dolores hung up the phone, she came over to me, wanting to know what the hell was going on. And that's when I finally told her: "He abused me, too."

---

[3] *In addition to my paranoia, I was supersensitive when anyone touched my children, even if it was done innocently. For example, I remember one of Dolores's relatives tickling my daughters. I found this upsetting and told him to stop. He didn't realize I was serious — what's wrong with tickling, right? — and he continued. I got so disturbed that I went into the kitchen to find Dolores. "Tell him to stop or I'll lay him flat on the ground," I said. Dolores, always the diplomat, got him to stop without ruffling his feathers.*

I don't remember what either of us said after that, but I do remember thinking to myself, "How could I have ever let that man into my house? What was I *thinking?*" I wouldn't have to answer that question again. I barred Uncle Johnny from my house. He would never go near my children again, or me.

CHAPTER 7
Hail Mary #1

I stopped farming in 1985. Although I was still in great shape, I noticed how the bodies of other farmers I knew were breaking down from all the hard physical work. I didn't want that to happen to me. Plus the money wasn't there, and Dolores and I had three children, with one more on the way. Because of our special relationship with Courtenay Jenkins, who died of cancer in 1985, and his wife, Muffie, we were allowed to stay on; in fact, we were given a lifelong lease. But after Muffie died in 1998, we decided to build our own place and left the farm for good in 1999, even though the Jenkins' son Courty extended his wishes that we stay on.

Years earlier, Courtenay got me into a men's prayer group. This was no ordinary group of men, however. They were

Baltimore blue bloods, very wealthy and successful businessmen. I was the youngest in the group and certainly the poorest, but they made me feel welcome and we became close over the years.

One day, I got to talking with group member Herman Stump, of Stump, Harvey and Cook Insurance in Hunt Valley, Maryland, which was close to where we lived. I was trying to figure out what my next move after farming would be, and I was toying around with the idea of returning to teaching Scout leadership training. I remember Herman and I sitting on his screened-in back porch when he suggested I go into the insurance business. "Nah," I said. "It's not for me." He asked why and I told him that I liked being my own man and how no two days in farming were alike. "Same thing as insurance," he said, and after a while he convinced me.

I worked for Herman until 1988, when his company was bought out by Corron & Black. I then went to work for Charter Group, the 74th largest agency in the country. The company had more than 100 employees, and I ran the sales division. Within 16 months I became the company's president and chief operating officer.

Ultimately, I decided to go out on my own, and in 1992, my friend Bill Chambers and I founded Coffey & Chambers, a full service brokerage firm. Bill had also worked for Corron & Black, and he returned to the company after he and I parted ways in 1994. I decided to stay and grow Coffey & Company, and as with farming, I gave it my all.[1] Since 1994, we have

---

[1] *Coffey & Company also introduced me to the corporate world of the many outstanding leaders who feel a calling to build something they can be passionate about. Their calling goes way beyond their companies, however. They also are passionate about using their talents and resources to change the lives of others, particularly those in need. Their vision and generosity of spirit have been inspiring and of immeasurable value in the founding and evolution of my not-for-profit, No More Stolen Childhoods.*

grown from $1 million in premiums to $22 million and today are recognized industry-wide for our service, integrity, professionalism and competence.

Needless to say, back in 1994, I was on top of the world professionally. Personally, I was imploding. Like a black hole, I was sucking my family into my continued rage. Dolores tried to get me to get help, but I refused. I thought I could handle my inner demons by myself, and the more she brought it up, the more stubborn I became. Finally, she had had it. Living with me had become too difficult; more so, she was no longer willing to be a buffer between the children and me. The kids didn't deserve my anger. Even when I wasn't angry, I rode them hard. If they didn't do things the way I thought they should be done, I'd give them a certain look or use a certain tone that was demeaning and scary. Dolores had every reason to say "no more," and that's when, unbeknownst to me, she sent out her first Hail Mary.

Although I refer to it as a Hail Mary, it only partly refers to the prayer for intercession recited in the Roman Catholic and Eastern Orthodox traditions. Hail Mary is also a football term for a forward pass made in desperation when a game is on the line. The chances of your receiver catching it are slim, but you throw the ball anyway because you've got no other options. Dolores had no other options when she threw out her Hail Mary. She prayed that someone, something — anything — step forward to help me. The very next day, her call was answered.

I remember it was a Thursday. I was driving to a meeting, listening to the radio show "Family Life Today," when I heard an interview with Dr. Dan B. Allender, who was a Biblical counselor and author of several books, including The Wounded Heart: Hope for Adult Victims of Childhood Sexual Abuse. Was this a coincidence? Divine intervention? Allender spoke about the damage of abuse — the feelings of powerlessness, unworthiness and betrayal it engenders, and how keeping abuse secret deadens the soul and negatively affects all relationships, including one's relationship to God. As I listened, I made two big decisions: I would seek counseling, and I would prosecute my Uncle Johnny for the crime he had committed against me. I went home that night and told Dolores. Her Hail Mary prayer had been answered.

I began counseling with Monsignor Michael Schleupner, who had baptized our children and whom I consider a true holy man, a modern-day shaman. I then began working with Dr. Rosalie Rappaport. She and I met weekly, and I came to understand just how deeply childhood sexual abuse wounds the soul and psyche. It's not something you get over because you've done counseling. The experience is who you are, and no amount of talking will change that. Lack of trust and self-esteem — these issues last a lifetime. And let's not forget the black hole of rage. It is like a deep cut that heals but will always leave a scar.

From that point on, I vowed to not keep Dolores in the dark about what I was feeling and to better control my mood swings, especially around the children. Things got better for a while, and that was no small feat.

Taking Uncle Johnny to court wasn't easy. Justifiably, Dolores had concerns. She knew it would be like opening a Pandora's box: emotions and family secrets would be bared. Further, my "coming out" to friends, colleagues and clients, not to mention my kids, would have consequences. Who knew what they would think or how they would respond?

They were right, of course, but I had to do it anyway. You could say it was my destiny. There was no way I could let Uncle Johnny get away with what he had done to me, especially after I learned he had abused another family member. I was also convinced he had victimized other children within (and likely outside) my extended family.[2] I couldn't stand by and let him continue to steal their childhoods.

By this time, I had told my mother and father about Uncle Johnny. I'll never forget how angry she got — not at her brother but at me. It was as if *I* were sullying the family's reputation, as if the family had not *already* been sullied. As to my father's reaction, he just sat in dumbfounded silence. Not then or for the rest of his life did he ever talk about Uncle Johnny's abuse. I could see from his face how upset it made him, but, as usual, he went along with whatever my mother wanted, which in this case was to say and do nothing.

In October of 1998, I filed a formal complaint with the Baltimore County Police Department, which seemed determined to make me feel like crap. No empathy, no compassion, just a bunch of questions: "Why didn't you come forward sooner?" "Did he *really* do XYZ or do you just *think* he did?" "Did you ever try to make him stop?" "Are you sure you want to go through with this? The guy's old now, you know." (As if age would stop Uncle Johnny or any other pedophile.)

When they realized I was serious, they told me the next step would be to bring in Uncle Johnny and see if he confessed. They did just that.[3] He didn't fight the charges or even get defensive. "If Wayne said it happened, it happened," he told the police.

As you may recall, Johnny was about 50 percent deaf. That meant he had to have a sign language interpreter on hand. That interpreter, it turned out, was my mother. I learned of this later

---

[2] *Statistics prove this to be a correct assumption. About 80 percent of all childhood offenders have one to nine victims; about 20 percent have 10 to 40 victims.*

[3] *I was not allowed to be present for this.*

and was flabbergasted and terribly hurt. How could she have chosen Johnny over me, her son? "Why are you doing this?" she asked me when I told her I would be pressing charges. "You have a great family, home and business." Did she really believe that my success in life should wipe the slate clean?[4]

I told the Maryland State's Attorney, Mr. John Cox, who would be representing me in court, that I didn't want Uncle Johnny's "blood money." Punitive damages couldn't buy back my childhood or remove my scars. Nor did I press for jail time. I simply wanted my uncle to take responsibility for his actions. I wanted my day in court. It came on May 10, 1999.

---

[4] *My mother may have opposed my sharing family secrets, but she had no problem keeping secrets of her own. Just as she didn't tell me she would serve as her brother's interpreter, she didn't tell me that Uncle Glen would defend Uncle Johnny, or that my Aunt Martha would be present at the trial to support Johnny. I didn't learn of this until moments before the trial began.*

CHAPTER 8
Dear Uncle John

January 4, 1999. Four months before trial.

Dear Uncle John:

I have been attending counseling for over a year now to deal with the effects of being abused sexually by you when I was a child. Since that abuse occurred, I have had to deal with shame, denial, betrayal and powerlessness. It has taken me many years to finally understand its effects and the impact it has had on my family. They have paid a heavy price for your actions and, unfortunately, will continue to pay until I have been able to come to some level of peace within myself.

No excuse can be given by you to negate the harm you caused when I was a child. You, in essence, stole my childhood and left a scar that will never go away. Your actions caused me to contact the authorities to reveal your abuse, with the hope and desire that the power of the law will be utilized to prevent you from molesting another child.

It has been difficult, as I stated, for my family and me. I have spoken to my wife, my oldest daughters and my parents to try to make them understand why I acted as I did and to ask for their forgiveness for my strange behavior at times — behavior that was rooted in what happened when you molested me. Through counseling and research into childhood sexual abuse, I now understand why I behaved the way I did.

Rest assured that I will rise above your abuse and seek every way possible to make sure that you face the consequences of your actions. In addition, I will tell my story to those in our family, as well as in the community at large, to bring to light the sickness of childhood sex abuse and the long-term damage to a child, at the time and in the future.

The time may come when you fully comprehend what pain you have caused my family and me. When that time does come, it is my hope you can reconcile with God and yourself.

Sincerely,
Wayne

CHAPTER 9
The Verdict

May 10, 1999. Baltimore County Circuit Court. State of Maryland vs. John Joseph Sprainis. The trial begins.

Present in the Court:

Thomas J. Bollinger, presiding judge
Attorney John Cox, on behalf of the State of Maryland
Attorney Russell White, on behalf of the defendant
Attorney Glen W. Trimmer, my uncle, on behalf of the defendant

    Mr. Cox: With the Court's permission, at this time I will call State versus John Sprainis, 99-CR-0119. John Cox present on behalf of the State.

Mr. White: Russ White. Good morning, your Honor. I represent Mr. Sprainis. He is mildly retarded, [has] 55 percent hearing loss. His brother-in-law, who is also an attorney, is going to assist [as a sign language interpreter].

Mr. Trimmer: Glen W. Trimmer.

Judge Bollinger: Yes. I understand the State has no objection to Mr. Trimmer helping as an interpreter.

Mr. Cox: That's correct. I have no reason to question he would not accurately interpret.

Judge Bollinger: I know you are an officer of the court, [but] we still have to swear you in as an interpreter for the record. Mr. DeWaters, swear him in.

Mr. Trimmer is sworn in.

From the back, I strain to hear. The experience is surreal. My stomach is in knots. Forty years of built-up emotions are now pulled and twisted together.

I am so glad Dolores and Katie are with me; I couldn't handle this alone. And it's good to have Father Chase of Illuminations here, too. His organization works with abuse victims, so he understands how hard it is for me to be here.

Judge Bollinger: Thank you. What's it going to be?

Mr. Cox: Your Honor, there have been plea negotiations, the substance of which [is that] the defendant will be pleading guilty to a charge within the charging document, upon the acceptance of the plea charge of perverted practice. The State affirms a suspended sentence, with specific conditions of probation.

> *I balk at the word "suspended," even though I chose not to press for a jail sentence for my uncle.*

Judge Bollinger: All right. Do you want to advise your client, Mr. White, slowly, so both the interpreter can handle the matter and [the stenographer] can get it down?

Mr. White: Your Honor, we have previously gone over it with him.

Mr. Trimmer: I have discussed this with Mr. Sprainis also.

Mr. White: For the record, we have to do it here at this [hearing].

Mr. Trimmer: Certainly.

Mr. White: Would you tell Mr. Sprainis he has the right to have a trial, either jury or court trial.

Mr. Trimmer: [Signs to the defendant.]

> *I am tempted to turn away. Signing is the primary way in which Uncle Johnny communicates. I, too, know how to sign, but I now find it hard to watch anyone use sign language; it causes flashbacks to my abuse.*

Mr. White: If he elects a jury trial, a jury is comprised of 12 persons selected from a larger group. We would have limited say in the selection of a jury.

Mr. Trimmer: He says he understands.

Mr. White: Several more things. When he pleads guilty, although the State is going to recommend a suspended sentence, Judge Bollinger is not bound by that recommendation.

> *Good. The judge can decide independently to impose a sentence or punitive damages. Surely he'll at least weigh the matter, given the heinous nature of my uncle's crime.*

Mr. Trimmer: [The defendant] understands that.

Mr. White: If he were to go to trial, he would have a right to testify himself, or he would have the right to remain silent. If he remains silent, the Court would instruct the jury that [the silence] could not be construed as evidence against him.

When he pleads guilty, his appeal rights are severely restricted. Normally, if he were tried by either a judge or jury and was found guilty, he would have an automatic right to appeal to the Court of Special Appeals. When he pleads guilty, he can only request the Court of Appeals to grant him the privilege of filing an appeal. That can only be one of four grounds.

One ground would be this Court doesn't have jurisdiction, like if this offense occurred in a different county. Another would be that the Court imposes a sentence beyond that authorized by law. The next would be that his attorney did not properly represent him. And I ask him, is he satisfied with my services at this time?

> *One ground, two grounds — what does it matter? Why do we have to drag this out? So Uncle Johnny can have his rights protected? What about mine?*

Mr. Trimmer: Yes.

Mr. White: The fourth and last would be that this plea was not voluntary. Has anybody promised him anything or threatened him, or in any way caused him to plead guilty other than the plea bargain that has been presented by the State?

Mr. Trimmer: No.

Mr. White: Has he had any medication or any type of drug, or anything that would affect his understanding today?

Mr. Trimmer: No.

Judge Bollinger: Thank you. Have a seat. I would like to hear the statement of facts.

> *I know it is the judge's job, his duty, to listen dispassionately to the facts, but I can't. "Facts," as he refers to them, are devoid of emotion or consequence. But for me, they are open wounds.*

Mr. Cox: Your Honor, a factual statement in support of the defendant's plea:

On the 13th of October, 1998, the Baltimore County Police were contacted by Wayne Coffey. He indicated there had been sexual contact between Mr. Coffey, date of birth April 20, 1954, with the defendant, John Joseph Sprainis, date of birth December 24, 1937. At the time of the contact, Mr. Coffey was a minor child under 18 years of age.

On the 15th of October 1998, Det. Raines of the Baltimore County Police met with Mr. Coffey at the Child Advocacy Center. [Mr. Coffey] advised [that] the abuse involved an uncle, occurred between the age of five and 13 years of age. It started with his uncle fondling his penis, Mr. Coffey's penis, [and] with Mr. Coffey having to fondle Mr. Sprainis' penis. Mr. Coffey having to perform oral sex on his uncle, and his uncle performing oral sex on him.

> *Hold it together, I tell myself, but it is hard. The State's Attorney is referring to me in the third person. He's talking about fondling and oral sex in front of all these people, including Dolores and Katie. How are they handling this? Should I really have brought them with me?*

Mr. Cox: The defendant constantly told him not to tell anyone. [Mr. Coffey stated] he finally put a stop to the abuse. [Mr. Coffey stated] his uncle constantly brought him gifts and took him everywhere.

On the 17th of November 1998, Detective Raines conducted an interview with John Sprainis, the defendant seated at [the] trial table, with [his] counsel to the left, at the Child Advocacy Center. The [defendant] was hearing impaired. Sgt. Ralph Bridges, also with Baltimore County Police, assisted with the interview.

Sgt. Bridges read the defendant his Miranda rights. [The defendant] advised he understood those rights and waived those rights, and agreed to speak to the detective through the use of sign language.

He admitted to touching Wayne Coffey's penis and having Wayne touch him. Asked about oral sex, he says, if Wayne says it happened, it must be true. He said he just doesn't remember. Mr. Sprainis believes William [Wayne] was about nine or ten years of age. It occurred approximately two, three times a month. [The defendant] advised it occurred whenever he would visit Wayne at his mother's house.

> *This is all so ridiculous. Uncle Johnny doesn't remember, even though he abused me for eight years? Or that the abuse also occurred all of those awful Sundays and holidays at my grandfather's house?*

All of the events occurred [within] Baltimore County, Maryland. That is the statement in support of the defendant's plea.

Judge Bollinger: Any additions, corrections, deletions or modifications?

Mr. White: No, your Honor.

Judge Bollinger: As to the statement?

Mr. White: No, sir.

Judge Bollinger: I find the plea is knowingly, voluntarily and intelligently given. The statement of facts supports the same. The verdict is guilty of article —

> *Intelligently given? He's making it seem as if Uncle Johnny is to be commended.*

Mr. White: Thank you, your Honor. Any information I can give the Court will be verified by Mr. Trimmer.
Mr. Sprainis is now 61 years of age. He was born December 24, 1937. He has always been single.

What does being single have to do with anything? That single people don't sexually abuse children, only married ones? I'd like to have Mr. White show me the research that supports this.

Mr. White: He attended the Maryland School for the Deaf, which, incidentally, is a place where he was molested. [I] have had some experience there; apparently, a lot of that goes on at that particular school.

Surely, it is terrible that my uncle was abused. But while it makes his behavior more understandable — the majority of abusers have been abused themselves — it doesn't absolve him of his crime. To understand is to not endorse.

Mr. White: [The defendant] is mildly mentally retarded, to a certain extent.

Wait a minute! Just seconds ago, the judge said Uncle Johnny's plea was intelligently given. Now my uncle's attorney is trying to curry favor by telling the court my uncle is mildly retarded "to a certain extent." Why doesn't he just tell the truth — that Uncle John is 50 percent mentally retarded, yes, but that he also is allowed to have a driver's license and his own car, and can live independently. If he has the ability to do these things, he also has the ability to commit sexual abuse.

Mr. White: He works at the Naval Academy. He worked there 23 years. He works in the kitchen, making salads. Does pots and pans, things like that at the Naval Academy.

Apparently since that time, there has been no tendency to pedophilia-type thing. He has been free of any type of activity like that ...

> *How can my uncle's attorney state this as fact? After all, no one knew about what he did to me or to other members of my family. And as to the pedophilia-type thing — he is around grown men at the Naval Academy, not young children.*

... never been arrested before, never charged with a crime. Of course, never been convicted of anything. He has no prior arrests of any type. He is now in therapy. Mr. Trimmer, you are a little bit more familiar with that than I am. Where does he do his therapy?

Mr. Trimmer: Well, I'm not familiar where he goes for therapy, but I understand he has been going to therapy, your Honor.

Mr. White: I'm sorry. He is treated by Mr. Ron Gompf. ... He is being treated by him. Can you ask him how long he has been?

Mr. Trimmer: Four, five times he has gone there.

> *Four or five times? That's absurd. And what kind of therapist is Mr. Gompf anyway? Is he qualified to work with pedophiles?[1] Does he believe Uncle Johnny is miraculously cured and can now be let loose on the street?*

---

[1] *As I later learned, Mr. Gompf was not a therapist who specialized in treating pedophiles. Rather, he was an alcohol and drug counselor.*

Mr. White: So, he deeply regrets this happened. He admitted it very promptly when confronted with it, Judge. I really doubt seriously whether he would be any type of risk in the future.

Apparently, he has an impeccable reputation. This is the only blemish he has had.

The only blemish? Sexual abuse isn't a blemish. It's a despicable crime.

Mr. Cox: No penitentiary, misdemeanor.

Mr. White: I would ask your Honor to grant him probation before judgment.

Judy Bollinger: [Does the] State wish to be heard?

Mr. Cox: Yes, your Honor. I apologize. I omitted to sharing this with Mr. White — Mr. Coffey is present.

To be perfectly frank, when the case originally was reported, I was contacted by detectives. Then I contacted Mr. Coffey. With the age of the offense, [and the] prospect of what could result, Mr. White is right. This is the [defendant's] first foray into the criminal justice system.

Mr. Coffey knows about other incidents within the family, but his main concern also [has] been reiterated to me today, [to] assure this could not happen again. I'm personally a little bit concerned. All we have is a representation or a name of a [therapist] he is seeing.

I would feel more comfortable with some sort of evaluation, at least try as much as humanly possible to assure there is not an existent problem — what the prospect of the counseling he is apparently in right now [would be].

Surely the judge has to agree on the need for an evaluation. How could he not?

I would hand up a victim impact statement from Mr. Coffey.

This is the statement I filed with the Court. I listen intently, hoping the judge will understand that the justice I seek is not unreasonable.

As I said, it is Mr. Coffey's primary concern to assure this will not happen again. That's why he never had any desire to ask for any incarceration. In this particular circumstance, we would ask that you impose a suspended sentence; place [the defendant] on probation, with the condition, obviously, he continue with any and all treatment that he is currently receiving and any deemed appropriate by parole and probation — that Mr. Gompf's [treatment be] appropriate or what is necessary in this particular circumstance, in the estimation of any supervising probation agent.

I would also ask, as reflected in the victim impact statement, [that he defendant] be directed to have no contact with Mr. Coffey or his family, or through [Mr. Coffey's] business.

Mr. White: Judge, all those things could be done and still grant probation before judgment.

Judge Bollinger: Well, I'm impressed. I know nothing about the therapist. I know an awful lot about [the] United States Navy.

Impressed? What does this mean? That working at the Naval Academy makes one a model citizen, above reproach? And why doesn't he want to know something about the therapist? Requiring Uncle Johnny to see a therapist was the one condition under which his probation was to be granted. That's all I ever asked for.

Judge Bollinger: Do they know anything about this? He has had no problems in the Naval Academy in 23 years?

Mr. White: Nothing, Judge.

Judge Bollinger: All right. Well, anything he wishes to say?

Mr. White: He will remain silent.

Judge Bollinger: All right. Grant judgment under Article 27, Section 641 — a probation period of three years. Condition of probation is to continue with the therapy he is now in and until discharged. And there will be no contact with Mr. Coffey and/or his family in any means whatsoever.

This is not a 792 situation?

Mr. Cox: No, not at all.

Judge Bollinger: All right.

Clerk: Costs, Judge?

Mr. White: Thank you, your Honor.

Judge Bollinger: I'll waive the costs.

Clerk: Do you want it to be supervised probation?

Judge Bollinger: Unsupervised.

Unsupervised! That's not even a slap on the hand.

We have to advise him of his rights. If you would be so kind, [Mr. Trimmer], would you repeat what I say?

Mr. Trimmer: I will try my best.
Let me say I did advise him of his rights prior to coming to court today. So did Mr. White. He comprehends what it is about. It is rather difficult to get the criminal justice system conveyed to a gentleman with his degree of intellect.

A gentleman? Degree of intellect? Are we playing that card again? Come on now — do you really need a high I.Q. to understand that abusing children is wrong?

Mr. White: I had advised him. If he accepts that, which he does, he waives any right to appeal.

Mr. Trimmer: Absolutely, I discussed that with him.

The proceeding is concluded.

That's it. Nearly forty years after my uncle's abuse began, it is over. The day of reckoning has come and gone in less than 20 minutes. But can justice be that swift? Will I now stop having problems sleeping? Will I feel less angry and shameful? Will I stop believing I must be perfect at everything I do? Will I finally be more trusting of my wife's love or be able to show my children the affection they deserve?

I suppose I should be satisfied that Uncle Johnny has pled guilty. But now I realize it is not enough. At the very least, he should be forced, as a condition of his probation to be evaluated as a pedophile by a counselor trained in this field. He should also be forced to continue counseling, supervised counseling. If he is not supervised, he can stop seeing a therapist at any time — today even — and no one would know. He is under no obligation to change his ways.

And that means only one thing: I have tried but not succeeded in keeping other children safe from him. I must find another way to do so.

I will *find another way.*

CHAPTER 10
Dear Mom

Dear Mom:

I have thought about writing this letter for a long time but have had to deal with my fight to overcome what was a very difficult and painful part of my life — a part that for many years I buried, thinking that on my own I could resolve this issue. Unfortunately, as I grew older, the pain and nightmares become unbearable to continue in this vein.

What I have had to deal with is the sexual abuse as a child by your brother Johnny. I can no longer consider him my uncle or godfather, as he took advantage of our relationship from the time I was five until I was 13 years old. The ironic thing is that he was my godfather, and the family thought this was a wonderful thing. But for me, it was a time of shame and an overwhelming lack of self-esteem and heartache.

I wrote this letter to my mother around the time of Uncle Johnny's trial. My intent was to tell her everything I was thinking and feeling. I was seeking catharsis, yes, but I was also struggling to understand what had happened to me as a child, and why.

I hoped, as I admit still hope today, that my mother would finally acknowledge the terrible crime her brother had committed against me, not to mention another family member, perhaps even several. How could she not? Hadn't he confessed in court? So why was she still angry at *me*?

But the thing that hurts the most was my mother's insistence that our family "secret" remain a secret. By doing so, she, in essence, chose her brother over me, her flesh and blood. But wasn't I the one to suffer most, not to mention my wife and my children? As for Johnny — his unsupervised probation amounted to little more than a slap on the wrist.

> *I started counseling over a year ago to help me deal with what happened and to try to understand its impact on me as a person. The scars are deep and the shame is unbearable at times. I have learned to deal with this by trying to be an overachiever in everything I do. My childhood was one of always trying to please and to become the perfect child, of never believing that I had your love. Why else would you allow this to happen? Could you not see it?*

After I barred Uncle Johnny from my house, I told my mother I never wanted to see him again. I wouldn't tolerate his being around when I visited her. He disgusted me. I also told her that I did not want him anywhere near my dad's funeral or hers, for that matter. But when my father died, my mother snuck Johnny into the funeral home one night before visiting hours — the same night Dolores and I stopped by early to spend time alone with my Dad. You can only imagine my shock and dismay. Again she chose Johnny over me.

I know you have noticed that I have not been spending as much time at your home. The reason is that I have a sick feeling every time I visit because of what took place in your house, the very house that should have been a safe haven for me as a child.

The sick feeling wasn't just psychological but physical, although it took a while for me to make the connection. Dolores and I would be coming back from a visit, and my stomach would begin to hurt, as if I had the beginnings of food poisoning. I couldn't understand it because I had been eating my mother's food all my life. Finally, I realized my body was telling me that I had to begin cutting ties to my birth family and what had once been my home. I have to tell you, if it burned to the ground tomorrow, it wouldn't bother me. It hurts to say that, though. Can you imagine yourself saying it about your childhood home — a home that held, or should have held, fond memories?

For all my talk, however, I know the ties to my mother are not so easily undone. They'll always be there, no matter how weak their pull. No matter how old I get, a part of me will always be the child who tries to make sense of things and who wonders what more he could have done to make his mother understand the deep scars her brother had left him with.

CHAPTER 11

Hail Mary #2 – Flag Is Up Farm

As I've noted, the scars of childhood sexual abuse run deep, but they also run wide. They extend to those you love most in the world. For me, this means Dolores and my very strong and loving children. Although my mood swings were less pronounced when I began counseling, my family continued to be the brunt of my anger. Counseling helped me understand the connection between my past and present. Unfortunately, I thought understanding alone was enough. I stopped my weekly counseling sessions, believing I had everything under control. Dolores knew otherwise.

She tried to get me back into counseling, but I wouldn't budge. Instead I slid back into my unpredictable, explosive ways. As before, Dolores tried to run interference between me and the children, protecting them from the very man who should have been their father. She could only do so much, however. She was wearing down and feeling emotionally bruised. The kids needed a less stressful environment, a better life. Still, I refused to get help. I was convinced I had it all under control.

One night at home, Dolores convinced me to watch the movie *Mystic River* starring Timothy Robbins. Robbins plays Dave, who, as a boy, is abducted by strangers and sexually assaulted. I didn't know a whole lot about the movie, so I was caught unawares when Dave was whisked away. To see his petrified face — it drilled into my heart, mind and soul. All of the years of dammed up emotions were more than I could take. I ran into the kitchen, physically ill and emotionally spent, and began sobbing uncontrollably.

It was then that Dolores sent out her second Hail Mary. There was no more she could do for me. She — I — needed a miracle. One week later, her prayers were answered.

It was 2004 and we were out in California, on a professional retreat for insurance executives. There were about 200 of us, including our spouses, and we took a day trip to a place called Flag Is Up Farm in Solvang, in Santa Barbara County.[1] There, we were to watch a guy named Monty Roberts break a wild mustang using a method he developed called Join-Up.

Monty was a legend, the original horse whisperer.[2] He went all over the world, training, speaking and working with horses, including Queen Elizabeth's. He also hosted retreats like ours for the leadership teams of powerhouse companies like Disney, Chrysler, Citibank and Oracle. No slouch this guy.

Monty didn't actually whisper to horses as much as communicate in their own language, which he called Equus.

---

[1] *"Flag is up" is a horse racing term that refers to the moments before a race begins. The flag is up as horses take their positions in the gate. Once the flag drops, the race begins and official timing starts.*

[2] *In fact, the Robert Redford movie "The Horse Whisperer" was inspired in part by Monty, who served as an advisor to the film.*

Monty believed that if you could get on a horse's wavelength, earn its trust, you didn't have to break it the traditional way, which was, in essence, to bully or use violence to force the horse into submission. Through Join-Up, a horse would turn into a puppy dog that followed its trainer around, all in 30 minutes. Yeah, right.

As a former farmer who had lived for years around horses, I wasn't buying. I knew you had to show a horse who was boss. So I watched skeptically from the bleachers as Monty did his thing, telling all around me that he had worked with the horse before that day.

Later that night, we had a barbeque on the farm, and Monty went from table to table, chatting. Mine was the last table he approached, and I expressed my skepticism and debated him for a good 15 minutes on his techniques. I was a bit combative, downright rude, as Dolores said later.

When Dolores told me this, I sought Monty out among the crowd and apologized. I told him I believed he had a gift with horses but that I had been around some tough horses in my life and didn't think his Join-Up technique would work on them. We talked for a few minutes, and then he asked if I had another minute. I said I did, and he walked me into his magnificent home, through his living room and down a hallway filled with pictures, halters and awards for his work with horses. Finally, he stopped, turned to me and stated, "Here is my guest bedroom. I'm asking you back as my guest. I'd like to teach you something. I'd like you to try the Join-Up technique for yourself." I can't remember exactly what I said in response, but it was probably polite but noncommittal. After that, I rejoined my group.

About an hour later, unbeknownst to me, Monty pulled Dolores aside. "Your husband's in trouble," he told her. "I want you to do all you can to get him back here for a weekend. I can help him." Dolores fell into his arms, crying. Three months later, we returned to Flag is Up Farm and, true to his word, Monty did help me. He was the wide receiver who caught Hail Mary #2.

Monty, it turned out, saw a lot of himself in me — the tension and bottled up rage. He, too, had been abused as a boy, not sexually, but physically by his father, who whipped him with chains. By the time he was 12, he had had 72 broken bones.

During our return visit, we spent four incredible days together. Our days were spent working with horses and our nights talking for hours — Dolores and I, and Monty and his wife, Pat. Over breakfast the last morning, Monty said to me, "Each day, I wake up a violent man. Because of my experience with my violent father, violence is imprinted on me. But I make a decision not to stay that way. Not in a million years will I be forced to be violent. Instead, I wake up each morning determined to do some good." His admission affected me profoundly. You might say it startled my senses.

During my visit, I did what I had believed was impossible just three months prior. I stood in Monty's horse ring, a 1,200-pound wild mustang circling me, and, using Monty's technique had a Join-Up with the horse. It was a profound lesson in the importance — the incredible power — of trust.

As Monty and I continued our talks, we began in earnest to discuss ways I could use my experience and resources to help sexually abused children. And so the seeds of my not-for-profit, No More Stolen Childhoods, were planted. It was time for the farmer to sow seeds again.

CHAPTER 12
No More Stolen Childhoods

I strongly believe in God and His infinite wisdom. I don't know why things happened to me as they did, but I can't help but think this is all part of God's Divine Plan. I wouldn't be the person I am today had I not gone through what I did as a child. I wouldn't have become a Scout or farmer, nor would I have a successful insurance agency or made such great friends over the years. More importantly, I wouldn't have Dolores, my soul mate, or my dear children. I can't imagine where I'd be without them; surely, I would not be among the living.

I know now that God's plan includes my doing everything I can to protect children from being sexually abused. Speaking out about my experiences is central to this and my calling. But it hasn't been easy.

To share is to relive and it is painful. Maybe one day, I can distance myself enough from Uncle Johnny and those terrible

Sundays and holidays. For now, though, whenever I come home from a No More Stolen Childhoods presentation, I am wiped out physically and mentally. Dolores worries about me and sometimes wonders if it's all worth it. What she says makes sense, still ... .

To tell my story also requires that I let my guard down, and this goes against all business instincts. In the professional world, you've got to appear invulnerable. And so I get nervous about the perceptions of colleagues. Will they think less of me? Will their discomfort get in the way of our working together?

I do have to say, however, that I've gotten amazing support from most of them, especially those in my Vistage group.[1] When I came back from my long weekend with Monty Roberts, they were looking forward to hearing about my adventures. I told them about my joining up with the wild mustang and the long talks Monty and I had had. And then I told them about Uncle Johnny. When I was done, you could hear a pin drop. For a moment, I got nervous; clearly, they did not know what to say. But then their caring words poured out, and I knew all would be well. (In fact, one member now serves on the No More Stolen Childhood board.)

Which is not to say I am at peace with myself. Like Monty, I have a lot of anger and always will. Some days are rough. The past, like quicksand, sucks me in, and no matter how hard I struggle, I can't get out of it. I'm still not the husband and father I wish I were, and my sense of remorse is profound. Trusting others is difficult. Some days I work too long and hard, scared that if I slow down, bad memories will overtake me. Some nights, I can't sleep and retreat to my library to write in my journal or read a book that will change my mindset.

But I know this: My life is now mine. I have reclaimed it. There will be no more secrets, no more stolen childhoods, as long as God gives me the breath to breathe.

---

[1] *Vistage is an international organization that brings together in small groups, or chapters, CEOs from companies around the world. The goal is to share information and ideas, but, more so, to support each other personally and professionally.*

APPENDIX 1
No More Stolen Childhoods Pledge

- I believe that sexual abuse of children is wrong. I acknowledge that childhood sexual abuse is prevalent and pervasive.

- I understand that childhood sexual abuse is devastating and causes lasting damage to its victims.

- I support the victims of childhood sexual abuse, children and adults, as they seek healing and hope.

- I will protect the children in my life from childhood sexual abuse to the best of my ability by learning about the risks that lead to abuse and will always listen with respect to any child.

- In my family, work, community and wherever my life may take me, I am committed to supporting any initiatives, legislation, education or policies that further the fight against childhood sexual abuse.

- I stand against the secrets and silence that surround childhood sexual abuse. By signing this pledge, I raise my voice on behalf of all children who could not, or cannot, speak for themselves.

- I pledge to remain firm in the fight until the day that there are No More Stolen Childhoods.

APPENDIX 2
Facts About Childhood Sexual Abuse

What constitutes childhood sexual abuse?

Childhood sexual abuse is any sexual act with a child performed by an adult or older child. This act can include any or all of the following:

- Fondling a child's genitals
- Having a child fondle an adult's genitals
- Mouth to genital contact
- Rubbing an adult's genitals on a child
- Penetrating the child's vagina or anus
- Showing an adult's genitals to a child
- Showing the child pornographic pictures or movies
- Using the child as a model to make pornographic material

How prevalent is childhood sexual abuse?
There are approximately 39 million survivors of childhood sexual abuse in America today.
- 1 in 4 girls and 1 in 6 boys are abused before age 18.
- The median age for reported abuse is 9 years old.
- 1 in 5 children are solicited sexually while on the Internet.
- More than 50 percent of abused children are abused by a family member or someone known to the family; an additional 40 percent are abused by older or larger children that they know.
- 70 percent of all reported sexual assaults occur to children ages 17 and under.
- 50 percent of all victims under 12 are victims of forcible sodomy, sexual assault with an object and/or forcible fondling.

Who are the perpetrators?
- 95 percent of abusers of girls are men; 80 percent of the perpetrators of boys are men.
- Many are married and have children of their own.
- Step-daughters are 8 times more likely at risk of being sexually abused.
- About 80 percent of childhood sexual abusers have between 1 and 9 victims; about 20 percent have 10 to 40 victims.
- The average serial child molester may have as many as 400 victims.

How do abusers operate?
- More than 80 percent of sexual abuse cases occur on a one-to-one basis.
- Abusers often become friendly with the child and the child's family.
- Abusers often seduce their victims over a 6- to 9-month period.

How willing are children to speak out about their abuse?

- More than 30 percent of victims never disclose their abuse to anyone.
- 80 percent of victims initially deny their abuse or are tentative in disclosing it.
- 75 percent of victims who tell others about their abuse do so accidentally.
- 20 percent of victims recant even though the abuse occurred.
- Only 1 to 4 percent of sexual abuse reports are fabricated.

Why don't more children come forward?

- Victims may not recognize their victimization as sexual abuse.
- Abused children may be too young to understand, let alone express, what is going on.
- Because children often know and trust their abusers, they can become trapped by loyalty, even affection, for the person.
- Abusers often force children to remain silent by threatening or shaming them, or by convincing them that the abuse is OK.
- Abusers often manipulate children into thinking that they are the guilty ones, and that their admission will make their parents angry or disappointed, or that it will disrupt, or even destroy, their families.

What are the long-term effects of childhood sexual abuse?

Effects among girls:

- Young girls who are sexually abused are more likely to develop eating and psychiatric disorders; alcohol and drug abuse in adulthood; and promiscuous and inappropriate sexual behaviors.
- 60 percent of teens' first pregnancies are preceded by molestation, rape or attempted rape.
- 75 percent of teenage girl prostitutes have been sexually abused.

Effects among boys:
- 70 percent of male survivors seek psychological treatment for substance abuse due to alcohol and drug-related problems, suicidal thoughts and/or attempted suicide.
- 70 percent exhibit violence towards others or obsessive work habits.

What are some signs of possible childhood sexual abuse?
- Unusual interest in, or avoidance of, sexual material
- Sleep problems
- Depression or withdrawal from friends and family
- Statements about their bodies
- Refusal to attend school
- A sudden change in behavior or extreme mood swings
- Fear of certain people, places or activities
- Unreasonable fear of physical exams
- Physical signs like redness, rashes, swelling, urinary tract infections

What is the best way to talk to children you suspect or know have been victimized?
- As noted, 75 percent of victims who tell others about their abuse do so accidentally. Those who do come forward are most apt to talk to people they trust and may first gauge someone's interest in, or concern about, them. Even then they may only share parts of their experience.
- Remain calm. Don't panic, overreact or blame them.
- Listen and reassure them. Praise them for coming forward.
- Help children get help.

What are some resources I should know about?
There are many excellent organizations on a national, state and local level. Among them:
- American Psychological Association
- American Academy of Child and Adolescent Psychology
- National Center for Missing and Exploited Children
- American Academy of Pediatrics
- U.S. Department of Justice
- Darkness2light.com
- Stopitnow.com

On the Internet:
The FBI has a "Crimes Against Children" Web site that links to the online registries of childhood sex offenders in all 50 states. These registries allow you to retrieve information about offenders' names, addresses and specific offenses.
http://www.fbi.gov/hq/cid/cac/registry.htm

In the Baltimore, Maryland, area:
- Metro Maryland Counseling, Dr. Doris Morgan
- The Baltimore Child Abuse Center
- The Woodbourne Center

There are also many excellent books on the subject:
- *The Wounded Heart* by Dan Allender
- *Victims No Longer* by Mike Lew
- *The Courage to Heal* by Ellen Bass and Laura Davis
- *Soul Murder* by Leonard Shengold, M.D.
- *The Sexually Abused Male* by Mic Hunter

What can I do to help prevent childhood sexual abuse?

- Do all you can to protect your children. Try to know where they are and with whom. Limit or oversee their Internet use. Keep the lines of communication open, so they can share their experiences with you. Watch for physical and behavioral warning signs. Follow your gut, should you believe something is wrong. Let your children know you care and will advocate on their behalf.
- Help raise the awareness of childhood sexual abuse by sharing this book with others.
- Make a commitment to ending this heinous crime by signing the No More Stolen Childhood Pledge on page 75. Get others to sign the pledge as well.
- Help support the efforts of No More Stolen Childhoods by making a tax-deductible contribution.
- Help No More Stolen Childhoods spread the word by inviting D. Wayne Coffey to speak to your organization, club, church or civic group.

No More Stolen Childhoods
P.O. Box 1553
Cockeysville, MD 21030
1-877-666-6735
www.NoMoreStolenChildhoods.org

APPENDIX 3
Seeking Help

Throughout this book, I have spoken about my permanently scarred life. My wish, however, is that you see the hope within my struggle and life.

Life. Having life. Those of us who have been abused know what I mean by having life. It is something we pursue daily but which seems out of reach, like a rope dangling before us. But is it truly beyond our grasp? I think not. I am a testament that the rope can be caught and that, with the support of others, it can be used to climb out of the abyss.

I know the effort isn't easy, just as I know my journey is mine alone. Likewise, you have your own path to travel. You will encounter many trials and demons along the way, so you must travel when you feel ready, willing and able. Nonetheless, I would like to offer some thoughts.

- Rather than block out your abuse, acknowledge it. Accept it as it is a part of you that will never disappear. Understand that you are not to blame for what happened. Your childhood was stolen from you; you could not prevent it.

- Seek out someone whom you trust, be it your significant other, pastor or a friend. Choose the right time and place and share your experience. Its release may feel overwhelming, but it can also be cathartic, even spiritual.

- Do not let your fears prevent or delay you from sharing. Do not worry about what you will say; it will come to you. Those of us who have been sexually abused have a unique ability to speak of the inner parts of our soul.

- Know, always, that there is beauty and love in the world that surpasses all understanding, and that you have a right to it. Know, too, that you are one of God's magnificent creations. In His infinite wisdom, He has a purpose for you, so reach out and take His hand. Begin your healing together and you will find purpose in your life.

Acknowledgements

When you have lived 53 years, you realize just how many people have had a positive influence on your life. To these important people, I want to say thanks. This book would not have been written without them; they helped create it. Should I forget the names of those who have touched me in some way, let me acknowledge them here and express my deepest affection for all they gave me.

My deepest affection also goes *to my soul mate, Dolores,* who has given me the strength to survive during so many times in my life. How I knew when I first saw her that she would be my anchor and rock, I can only attribute to God in His infinite wisdom.

To Vistage 130 (formerly TEC 130), which was, and *still is,* an important part of my life and my leadership development. Two deceased members had a particularly significant impact: *Fred Walpert* and *Steve Campbell.* I am also grateful to our group's first chair, *Bob Soady,* who believed in my ability and inspired me to excel.

To Jim Hogg and John McBeth, my dear close friends, with whom I would stand back-to-back in any fight.

To the Boy Scouts of America. The staff of Schiff Scout Reservation was unbelievable, in particular *Dwayne Bucko, Alvin C.C. West, Paul Bradshaw* and *Norm Long.* I also want to express my gratitude to *Norris Tingle,* who, as my Scoutmaster, gave me the opportunity to change my life. *Nenitco Lodge 130* also is to be acknowledged. Through its focus on American Indian lifestyle and beliefs, I gained hope and direction.

To Courtenay and Muffie Jenkins, who owned Melinda's Prospect Farm and hired me to manage it. To *Ralph Moats,* who managed the farm next to mine and generously gave his time and knowledge.

To Herman Stump, who threw out a "life-line" when I decided to stop farming and gave me my start in the insurance business; and *Bill Baird,* who came out to the farm one day after a prayer meeting and said: "How long are you going to hide under the bushel basket? God has given you talents and you need to go out and share them."

To Forrest Bramble, who challenged me to re-evaluate my life and has been a mentor ever since.

To the members of my men's prayer group, Brandon Gaines, Todd Guntner, Roland Harvey, Mike Fitzpatrick, Craig Willie, Mike Blair, Hunter McCullough and *Karl Kokinakois* — they have been a fortress for me.

To Dr. Lee Thayer, the guru of high-performance organizations. He revolutionized my thinking and helped me to reinforce my leadership beliefs and hone them.

To Hugh Mohler, who believed in me and took me under his wing, assisting in any way he could.

To my clients, carriers, vendors, and incredibly dedicated and exceptional staff at Coffey & Company. I am eternally grateful for their sharing my vision to change the insurance agency system through the tenets of integrity, professionalism and competence.

To my counselor, Doris Morgan, who, through her guidance, has fostered my healing and my calling to God's will.

To Dave and Terri DeCenzo, my dear friends, who will always be in our lives as Dolores and I continue our journey.

To Monty and Pat Roberts, who were the catalysts for the beginning of No More Stolen Childhoods.

To Beth Mende Conny, my partner in this book. She had the patience and perseverance to bring out of me my past and future to give you my story! We became two "peas in a pod."

To Sara Denham, who as my Reiki practitioner and massage therapist, supports my journey through her gift of healing.

To the board of No More Stolen Childhoods Dolores Coffey, Katie Coffey, Mike Fitzpatrick, Jim Hogg, Todd Jennings, Denis O'Donovan, Chris Desautelle and Mark Semanie.

Finally, I am eternally grateful to my God and Savior for my existence, and to the American Indians, whose traditions helped me survive. Achegim!

About the Author

D. Wayne Coffey is the founder and president of Coffey & Company, one of the premier insurance agencies in Maryland.

Wayne founded No More Stolen Childhoods in 2004, to increase public awareness of childhood sexual abuse and to help victims reclaim their lives. A victim himself, he today devotes much of his time to speaking before groups and leading workshops for troubled youths struggling to cope with their abuse.

Wayne resides in Reisterstown, MD, with Dolores, his wife of 32 years. He is the president of the Baltimore chapter of Legatus, a national organization of Catholic business owners, and is actively involved in Sacred Heart of Glyndon Church. He also serves as the chairman of the Bay National Bank's advisory board and several insurance companies' advisory boards.

His free time finds him enjoying the outdoors: hunting, hiking, golfing and shooting sporting clays.